# Pioneer Village

## Therese McNamara

**Literacy Consultants**
David Booth • Kathleen Corrigan

The pioneer village

shows life in the past.

In the past, some people lived on farms.

Some farms had sheep.

Sheep have wool.

Pioneers got wool

from sheep.

Pioneers put color
in the wool.

This is a spinning wheel.

Pioneers put wool

in the wheel.

The wheel made yarn.

This is a loom.

Pioneers put yarn

in the loom.

This made cloth.

They made things

with the cloth.

Pioneers made shirts
with the cloth.

There is a lot to see
at the pioneer village.